50 High-Protein Breakfast Recipes for Home

By: Kelly Johnson

Table of Contents

- Scrambled eggs with spinach and feta
- Greek yogurt parfait with berries and almonds
- Protein pancakes with cottage cheese
- Breakfast burrito with eggs, black beans, and avocado
- Omelette with turkey, mushrooms, and cheese
- Quinoa breakfast bowl with nuts and fruit
- Smoked salmon and cream cheese on whole grain toast
- Tofu scramble with vegetables
- Egg muffins with spinach and cheese
- Cottage cheese and fruit bowl
- Breakfast wrap with scrambled eggs and chicken sausage
- Protein smoothie with protein powder, spinach, and banana
- Peanut butter and banana on whole grain toast
- Chia seed pudding with almond milk and berries
- Egg white omelette with smoked salmon and dill
- Avocado toast with poached egg
- Protein waffles with Greek yogurt topping
- Turkey sausage and vegetable frittata
- Cottage cheese pancakes with berries
- Breakfast quinoa with nuts and honey
- Egg and vegetable stir-fry
- Greek yogurt with protein granola and sliced banana
- Spinach and cheese frittata
- Breakfast sandwich with egg, cheese, and turkey bacon
- Almond butter and banana smoothie
- Quinoa breakfast muffins with ham and cheese
- Protein oats with almond milk and sliced almonds
- Egg white breakfast burrito with salsa and avocado
- Cottage cheese and spinach omelette
- Greek yogurt pancakes with blueberries
- Breakfast salad with hard-boiled eggs and bacon
- Protein-packed French toast with strawberries
- Veggie and tofu scramble wrap
- Protein-packed overnight oats with chia seeds and nuts
- Turkey and cheese breakfast quesadilla

- Smoked salmon and avocado toast
- Protein-packed banana bread with nuts
- Egg white and spinach breakfast sandwich
- Breakfast pizza with eggs, spinach, and feta
- Greek yogurt with protein powder and sliced almonds
- High-protein breakfast cookies with oats and nuts
- Egg muffins with turkey sausage and peppers
- Cottage cheese and fruit smoothie
- Spinach and mushroom breakfast burrito
- Protein-packed breakfast quiche with bacon and cheese
- Greek yogurt parfait with granola and berries
- Breakfast scramble with chicken sausage and vegetables
- High-protein pumpkin pancakes with Greek yogurt topping
- Egg white and vegetable breakfast wrap
- Protein-packed banana split with Greek yogurt and nuts

Scrambled eggs with spinach and feta

Ingredients:

- 4 large eggs
- 1 cup fresh spinach leaves, chopped
- 1/4 cup crumbled feta cheese
- 1 tablespoon butter or olive oil
- Salt and pepper to taste
- Optional: chopped fresh herbs such as parsley or dill for garnish

Instructions:

Crack the eggs into a mixing bowl and whisk them together until well combined. Season with salt and pepper to taste.
Heat the butter or olive oil in a non-stick skillet over medium heat.
Once the butter is melted or the oil is hot, add the chopped spinach to the skillet. Cook for 1-2 minutes, stirring occasionally, until the spinach is wilted.
Pour the whisked eggs into the skillet with the spinach. Allow the eggs to cook undisturbed for a minute or two until they start to set around the edges.
Use a spatula to gently push the eggs from the edges towards the center of the skillet, allowing the uncooked eggs to flow to the bottom of the pan.
Continue cooking and gently stirring the eggs until they are mostly set but still slightly runny.
Sprinkle the crumbled feta cheese evenly over the eggs.
Continue cooking for another minute or two, stirring gently, until the eggs are fully cooked and the feta cheese has softened.
Remove the skillet from the heat and transfer the scrambled eggs with spinach and feta to serving plates.
Garnish with chopped fresh herbs, if desired.
Serve the scrambled eggs immediately, with toast, sliced avocado, or your favorite breakfast sides.

Enjoy your delicious scrambled eggs with spinach and feta! It's a quick and easy meal that's packed with protein and flavor.

Greek yogurt parfait with berries and almonds

Ingredients:

- 1 cup Greek yogurt (plain or vanilla-flavored)
- 1/2 cup mixed berries (such as strawberries, blueberries, raspberries, or blackberries), washed and sliced if necessary
- 2 tablespoons sliced almonds
- 1-2 tablespoons honey or maple syrup (optional, for sweetness)
- Granola (optional, for extra crunch)

Instructions:

Start by layering the ingredients in a glass or bowl. Begin with a spoonful of Greek yogurt at the bottom of the glass.

Add a layer of mixed berries on top of the yogurt. You can use any combination of berries you like, or a single type of berry if preferred.

Sprinkle a tablespoon of sliced almonds over the berries.

If desired, drizzle a little honey or maple syrup over the almonds for added sweetness. This step is optional, especially if you're using flavored yogurt.

Repeat the layering process with the remaining yogurt, berries, and almonds until you've filled the glass or bowl. You can create as many layers as you like, depending on the size of your serving container.

If you prefer added texture and flavor, sprinkle a layer of granola between the yogurt and berries or on top of the parfait.

Garnish the top of the parfait with a few extra berries and almonds for a beautiful presentation.

Serve immediately and enjoy your delicious Greek yogurt parfait with berries and almonds!

Feel free to customize this recipe to suit your taste preferences. You can use different types of yogurt (such as regular or dairy-free yogurt), switch up the fruits or nuts, and adjust the sweetness level according to your liking. This parfait is not only delicious but also packed with protein, fiber, vitamins, and antioxidants, making it a nutritious choice to start your day or satisfy your cravings for a healthy snack.

Protein pancakes with cottage cheese

Ingredients:

- 1 cup old-fashioned oats
- 1 cup cottage cheese
- 2 large eggs
- 1 teaspoon vanilla extract
- 1/2 teaspoon baking powder
- 1/4 teaspoon cinnamon (optional)
- Pinch of salt
- Cooking spray or butter, for greasing the skillet
- Toppings of your choice (such as fresh berries, sliced bananas, maple syrup, honey, or nut butter)

Instructions:

Place the old-fashioned oats in a blender or food processor and pulse until they are finely ground to create oat flour.

Add the cottage cheese, eggs, vanilla extract, baking powder, cinnamon (if using), and a pinch of salt to the blender or food processor with the oat flour. Blend until smooth and well combined, scraping down the sides of the blender or food processor as needed.

Preheat a non-stick skillet or griddle over medium heat. Lightly grease the skillet with cooking spray or butter.

Once the skillet is hot, pour about 1/4 cup of the pancake batter onto the skillet for each pancake. Use the back of a spoon or a spatula to spread the batter into a circle if needed.

Cook the pancakes for 2-3 minutes on one side, or until bubbles start to form on the surface and the edges begin to set.

Flip the pancakes and cook for an additional 1-2 minutes on the other side, or until golden brown and cooked through.

Transfer the cooked pancakes to a plate and repeat the cooking process with the remaining batter, greasing the skillet as needed between batches.

Serve the protein pancakes warm with your favorite toppings, such as fresh berries, sliced bananas, maple syrup, honey, or nut butter.

Enjoy your delicious and nutritious protein pancakes made with cottage cheese!

These pancakes are high in protein and fiber, making them a satisfying and wholesome breakfast option. Feel free to customize the recipe by adding other ingredients like cocoa powder, protein powder, or spices to suit your taste preferences.

Breakfast burrito with eggs, black beans, and avocado

Ingredients:

- 4 large eggs
- 1 tablespoon butter or olive oil
- Salt and pepper to taste
- 1/2 cup canned black beans, drained and rinsed
- 1 avocado, sliced
- 4 large flour tortillas
- Salsa, for serving (optional)
- Shredded cheese (such as cheddar or Monterey Jack), for serving (optional)
- Chopped fresh cilantro, for garnish (optional)

Instructions:

Crack the eggs into a mixing bowl and whisk them together until well combined. Season with salt and pepper to taste.

Heat the butter or olive oil in a skillet over medium heat. Once hot, add the whisked eggs to the skillet.

Cook the eggs, stirring occasionally, until they are scrambled and cooked to your desired doneness. Remove from heat and set aside.

Warm the black beans in a small saucepan over medium-low heat, stirring occasionally, until heated through. Remove from heat and set aside.

To assemble the breakfast burritos, lay out the flour tortillas on a flat surface.

Divide the scrambled eggs evenly among the tortillas, placing them in the center of each tortilla.

Top the scrambled eggs with the warmed black beans and sliced avocado.

If desired, add a spoonful of salsa and a sprinkle of shredded cheese on top of the filling ingredients.

Fold the sides of each tortilla over the filling, then roll it up tightly from the bottom to create a burrito.

Optional: Heat a large skillet over medium heat and lightly toast each assembled burrito on all sides until golden brown and crispy.

Serve the breakfast burritos warm, garnished with chopped fresh cilantro if desired.

Enjoy your delicious breakfast burritos with eggs, black beans, and avocado! They're perfect for a hearty breakfast on the go or a leisurely weekend brunch.

Feel free to customize the recipe by adding other ingredients such as cooked bacon or sausage, diced tomatoes, sliced bell peppers, or jalapeños to suit your taste preferences.

Omelette with turkey, mushrooms, and cheese

Ingredients:

- 2 large eggs
- 1/4 cup cooked turkey, diced
- 1/4 cup mushrooms, sliced
- 1/4 cup shredded cheese (cheddar, mozzarella, or your choice)
- Salt and pepper to taste
- 1 tablespoon butter or oil for cooking
- Optional: chopped fresh herbs such as parsley or chives for garnish

Instructions:

Crack the eggs into a bowl and beat them lightly with a fork or whisk. Season with salt and pepper to taste.
Heat a non-stick skillet over medium heat and add the butter or oil.
Once the butter has melted or the oil is hot, add the diced turkey and sliced mushrooms to the skillet. Cook, stirring occasionally, until the mushrooms are tender and the turkey is heated through, about 3-4 minutes.
Spread the turkey and mushroom mixture evenly across the skillet and pour the beaten eggs over the top.
Allow the eggs to cook undisturbed for a minute or two until the edges start to set.
Using a spatula, gently lift the edges of the omelette and tilt the skillet to let any uncooked egg mixture flow underneath.
Once the eggs are mostly set but still slightly runny on top, sprinkle the shredded cheese evenly over one half of the omelette.
Carefully fold the other half of the omelette over the cheese to form a half-moon shape.
Cook for another minute or so until the cheese is melted and the eggs are cooked through to your desired doneness.
Slide the omelette onto a plate and garnish with chopped fresh herbs if desired.
Serve hot and enjoy your delicious turkey, mushroom, and cheese omelette!

Feel free to adjust the ingredients and seasonings according to your taste preferences.

Enjoy your meal!

Quinoa breakfast bowl with nuts and fruit

Ingredients:

- 1/2 cup quinoa, rinsed
- 1 cup water or milk of your choice (such as almond milk, coconut milk, or dairy milk)
- 1/4 teaspoon ground cinnamon (optional)
- 1/4 teaspoon vanilla extract (optional)
- Pinch of salt
- 1/4 cup mixed nuts (such as almonds, walnuts, pecans), chopped
- 1/2 cup fresh fruit (such as berries, sliced bananas, diced apples, or any fruit of your choice)
- 1 tablespoon honey or maple syrup (optional, for sweetness)
- Greek yogurt or coconut yogurt (optional, for serving)

Instructions:

Rinse the quinoa under cold water using a fine-mesh sieve to remove any bitter coating.

In a saucepan, combine the rinsed quinoa, water or milk, ground cinnamon (if using), vanilla extract (if using), and a pinch of salt. Bring to a boil over medium heat.

Once boiling, reduce the heat to low, cover, and simmer for about 15 minutes, or until the quinoa is cooked and the liquid is absorbed. Remove from heat and let it sit covered for a few minutes.

Fluff the quinoa with a fork and divide it into serving bowls.

Top each bowl of quinoa with the chopped mixed nuts and fresh fruit.

Drizzle with honey or maple syrup if desired for extra sweetness.

If using, add a dollop of Greek yogurt or coconut yogurt on top.

Serve warm and enjoy your nutritious and tasty quinoa breakfast bowl!

You can customize this breakfast bowl with your favorite nuts and fruits, and adjust the sweetness according to your preference. It's a great way to start your day with a healthy and satisfying meal!

Smoked salmon and cream cheese on whole grain toast

Ingredients:

- 2 slices of whole grain bread
- 2-4 ounces smoked salmon
- 2-4 tablespoons cream cheese
- Fresh dill, chopped (optional, for garnish)
- Lemon wedges (optional, for serving)
- Capers (optional, for serving)

Instructions:

Toast the slices of whole grain bread to your desired level of crispiness.
Once toasted, spread a layer of cream cheese evenly onto each slice of toast.
Place 1-2 ounces of smoked salmon on top of each slice of toast, arranging it evenly.
If desired, sprinkle some chopped fresh dill on top of the smoked salmon for added flavor.
Serve the smoked salmon and cream cheese toast with lemon wedges on the side for squeezing over the top, and capers for an extra burst of flavor.
Enjoy your delicious smoked salmon and cream cheese on whole grain toast as a satisfying breakfast, brunch, or snack!

Feel free to customize this recipe by adding other toppings such as sliced cucumbers, red onion, or avocado slices. It's a versatile and tasty dish that's perfect for any time of day!

Tofu scramble with vegetables

Ingredients:

- 1 block (about 14-16 ounces) firm tofu
- 1 tablespoon olive oil or cooking oil of your choice
- 1 small onion, diced
- 2 cloves garlic, minced
- 1 bell pepper, diced
- 1 cup mushrooms, sliced
- 1 cup spinach or kale, chopped
- 2 tablespoons nutritional yeast (optional, for added flavor)
- 1/2 teaspoon ground turmeric (for color and flavor)
- Salt and pepper to taste
- Optional: chopped fresh herbs such as parsley or chives for garnish

Instructions:

Start by pressing the tofu to remove excess water. Place the block of tofu on a plate lined with paper towels. Put another layer of paper towels on top of the tofu, then place a heavy object (like a skillet or a couple of cans) on top. Let it press for about 15-20 minutes while you prepare the vegetables.

Heat the olive oil in a large skillet over medium heat.

Add the diced onion and minced garlic to the skillet and sauté until softened and fragrant, about 2-3 minutes.

Add the diced bell pepper and sliced mushrooms to the skillet. Cook for another 3-4 minutes, or until the vegetables are tender.

Crumble the pressed tofu into the skillet using your hands or a fork, resembling scrambled eggs.

Add the chopped spinach or kale to the skillet and cook until wilted.

Sprinkle the nutritional yeast and ground turmeric over the tofu mixture. Stir well to evenly distribute the spices and incorporate them into the tofu.

Season the tofu scramble with salt and pepper to taste. Adjust seasoning as needed.

Continue cooking for another 2-3 minutes, stirring occasionally, until the tofu is heated through and any excess moisture has evaporated.

Remove the skillet from the heat. Garnish with chopped fresh herbs if desired.

Serve the tofu scramble hot, either on its own or with toast, tortillas, or alongside your favorite breakfast sides.

Enjoy your flavorful and satisfying tofu scramble with vegetables! It's a versatile dish that you can customize with your favorite veggies and spices.

Egg muffins with spinach and cheese

Ingredients:

- 6 large eggs
- 1 cup fresh spinach, chopped
- 1/2 cup shredded cheese (cheddar, mozzarella, or your choice)
- Salt and pepper to taste
- Cooking spray or oil for greasing the muffin tin

Instructions:

Preheat your oven to 350°F (175°C). Grease a 6-cup muffin tin with cooking spray or oil.

In a mixing bowl, crack the eggs and beat them lightly with a fork or whisk until well combined.

Stir in the chopped spinach and shredded cheese into the beaten eggs. Season with salt and pepper to taste.

Pour the egg mixture evenly into the greased muffin cups, filling each cup about 3/4 full.

Bake in the preheated oven for 20-25 minutes, or until the egg muffins are set and slightly golden on top.

Remove the muffin tin from the oven and let the egg muffins cool for a few minutes.

Using a butter knife or spatula, gently loosen the edges of the egg muffins and carefully remove them from the muffin tin.

Serve the egg muffins warm as a delicious and nutritious breakfast or snack.

These egg muffins with spinach and cheese are great for meal prep. You can store them in an airtight container in the refrigerator for up to 3-4 days. Simply reheat them in the microwave for a quick and easy breakfast on busy mornings. Enjoy!

Cottage cheese and fruit bowl

Ingredients:

- 1/2 cup cottage cheese
- 1/2 cup mixed fresh fruit (such as berries, sliced bananas, diced mango, or any fruit of your choice)
- 1 tablespoon honey or maple syrup (optional, for sweetness)
- 1 tablespoon chopped nuts (such as almonds, walnuts, or pecans) (optional, for added crunch)

Instructions:

Scoop the cottage cheese into a bowl.
Add the mixed fresh fruit on top of the cottage cheese.
If desired, drizzle honey or maple syrup over the fruit for added sweetness.
Sprinkle chopped nuts on top for added texture and flavor.
Gently toss the ingredients together, if desired, or leave them layered for a visually appealing presentation.
Serve immediately and enjoy your cottage cheese and fruit bowl!

This recipe is highly customizable, so feel free to adjust the types of fruit and toppings to suit your taste preferences. It's a nutritious and satisfying snack that's perfect for any time of day.

Breakfast wrap with scrambled eggs and chicken sausage

Ingredients:

- 2 large eggs
- 2 chicken sausages, sliced
- 2 large flour tortillas or whole wheat wraps
- 1/4 cup shredded cheese (cheddar, mozzarella, or your choice)
- Salt and pepper to taste
- 1 tablespoon olive oil or butter
- Optional toppings: sliced avocado, diced tomatoes, salsa, hot sauce, chopped fresh herbs

Instructions:

In a mixing bowl, crack the eggs and beat them lightly with a fork or whisk. Season with salt and pepper to taste.

Heat the olive oil or butter in a skillet over medium heat. Add the sliced chicken sausages to the skillet and cook until browned and heated through, about 4-5 minutes.

Once the sausages are cooked, push them to one side of the skillet and pour the beaten eggs into the other side.

Scramble the eggs gently with a spatula until they are cooked to your desired consistency.

Sprinkle shredded cheese evenly over the scrambled eggs and chicken sausages. Allow the cheese to melt slightly.

Warm the tortillas or wraps in the microwave or in a separate skillet for a few seconds to make them pliable.

Divide the scrambled eggs and chicken sausages evenly between the tortillas or wraps, placing the mixture in the center of each.

Add any optional toppings you like, such as sliced avocado, diced tomatoes, salsa, hot sauce, or chopped fresh herbs.

Fold the sides of each tortilla or wrap over the filling, then roll them up tightly to form a wrap.

Serve the breakfast wraps immediately, whole or sliced in half, and enjoy!

These breakfast wraps are perfect for a quick and satisfying morning meal. Feel free to customize them with your favorite ingredients and toppings.

Protein smoothie with protein powder, spinach, and banana

Ingredients:

- 1 scoop of your favorite protein powder (such as whey, soy, pea, or hemp protein)
- 1 ripe banana, peeled and sliced
- 1 cup fresh spinach leaves, washed
- 1 cup milk of your choice (such as dairy milk, almond milk, soy milk, or coconut milk)
- Optional add-ins: a handful of ice cubes, a spoonful of nut butter (such as almond butter or peanut butter), a drizzle of honey or maple syrup for sweetness

Instructions:

Place the protein powder, sliced banana, fresh spinach leaves, and milk in a blender.
If using, add any optional add-ins such as ice cubes, nut butter, or sweetener.
Blend on high speed until smooth and creamy, scraping down the sides of the blender as needed to ensure all ingredients are well incorporated.
Taste the smoothie and adjust the consistency or sweetness if desired by adding more milk or sweetener.
Once the smoothie reaches your desired consistency, pour it into glasses and serve immediately.
Enjoy your protein smoothie as a nutritious and delicious breakfast, snack, or post-workout refuel!

This protein smoothie is packed with protein, vitamins, and minerals from the protein powder, spinach, and banana. It's a great way to start your day or refuel after a workout while enjoying a tasty and satisfying drink. Feel free to customize the recipe by adding your favorite fruits or other nutritious ingredients.

Peanut butter and banana on whole grain toast

Ingredients:

- 2 slices of whole grain bread, toasted
- 2 tablespoons peanut butter (smooth or crunchy, your choice)
- 1 ripe banana, sliced
- Optional: honey or maple syrup for drizzling

Instructions:

Toast the slices of whole grain bread to your desired level of crispiness.
Spread 1 tablespoon of peanut butter evenly onto each slice of toast.
Arrange the sliced banana on top of the peanut butter, covering the entire surface of each slice.
If desired, drizzle honey or maple syrup over the bananas for added sweetness.
Serve the peanut butter and banana on whole grain toast immediately and enjoy!

This simple yet delicious combination of peanut butter and banana on whole grain toast is perfect for breakfast, a snack, or even a light meal. It's packed with protein, healthy fats, fiber, and vitamins, making it a nutritious and satisfying choice. Feel free to customize the recipe by adding toppings such as chia seeds, sliced strawberries, or a sprinkle of cinnamon for extra flavor and nutrition.

Chia seed pudding with almond milk and berries

Ingredients:

- 1/4 cup chia seeds
- 1 cup almond milk (or any milk of your choice)
- 1-2 tablespoons maple syrup or honey (optional, for sweetness)
- 1/2 teaspoon vanilla extract (optional, for flavor)
- Fresh berries (such as strawberries, blueberries, raspberries, or any berries of your choice) for topping
- Optional toppings: sliced almonds, shredded coconut, granola

Instructions:

In a mixing bowl or glass jar, combine the chia seeds, almond milk, maple syrup or honey (if using), and vanilla extract (if using). Stir well to combine all the ingredients.

Cover the bowl or jar and refrigerate the chia seed mixture for at least 2 hours, or preferably overnight, to allow the chia seeds to absorb the liquid and thicken into a pudding-like consistency. Stir the mixture occasionally during the first hour to prevent clumping.

Once the chia seed pudding has thickened to your desired consistency, remove it from the refrigerator.

Give the pudding a good stir to redistribute the chia seeds evenly.

Divide the chia seed pudding into serving bowls or glasses.

Top each serving with fresh berries and any other optional toppings you like, such as sliced almonds, shredded coconut, or granola.

Serve the chia seed pudding with almond milk and berries immediately, or store any leftovers in an airtight container in the refrigerator for up to 3-4 days.

Enjoy this creamy and nutritious chia seed pudding with almond milk and berries as a healthy breakfast, snack, or dessert option. It's rich in fiber, omega-3 fatty acids, and antioxidants, making it a satisfying and guilt-free treat!

Egg white omelette with smoked salmon and dill

Ingredients:

- 4 egg whites
- 2 ounces smoked salmon, thinly sliced
- 1 tablespoon fresh dill, chopped
- Salt and pepper to taste
- 1 teaspoon olive oil or butter

Instructions:

In a mixing bowl, whisk the egg whites until frothy. Season with salt and pepper to taste.
Heat the olive oil or butter in a non-stick skillet over medium heat.
Pour the whisked egg whites into the skillet and allow them to cook undisturbed for a minute or two until the edges start to set.
Using a spatula, gently lift the edges of the omelette and tilt the skillet to let any uncooked egg mixture flow underneath.
Once the egg whites are mostly set but still slightly runny on top, arrange the thinly sliced smoked salmon on one half of the omelette.
Sprinkle the chopped fresh dill over the smoked salmon.
Carefully fold the other half of the omelette over the smoked salmon and dill to form a half-moon shape.
Cook for another minute or so until the egg whites are fully cooked through and the omelette is heated through.
Slide the omelette onto a plate and garnish with extra dill if desired.
Serve hot and enjoy your delicious egg white omelette with smoked salmon and dill!

This omelette is light, flavorful, and packed with protein from the egg whites and smoked salmon. It's a perfect choice for a healthy and satisfying breakfast or brunch. Feel free to adjust the ingredients and seasonings according to your taste preferences.

Avocado toast with poached egg

Ingredients:

- 2 slices of whole grain bread, toasted
- 1 ripe avocado
- 2 large eggs
- Salt and pepper to taste
- Optional toppings: red pepper flakes, sliced tomatoes, crumbled feta cheese, chopped fresh herbs (such as cilantro or parsley)

Instructions:

Begin by preparing the poached eggs. Fill a medium-sized saucepan with water and bring it to a gentle simmer over medium heat.
Crack each egg into a small bowl or ramekin. This will make it easier to slide the eggs into the water.
Once the water is simmering, carefully slide each egg into the water, one at a time. Poach the eggs for about 3-4 minutes for a runny yolk, or longer if you prefer a firmer yolk.
While the eggs are poaching, prepare the avocado. Halve the avocado, remove the pit, and scoop the flesh into a bowl. Mash the avocado with a fork until smooth or slightly chunky, depending on your preference. Season with salt and pepper to taste.
Spread the mashed avocado evenly onto the toasted slices of whole grain bread.
Once the eggs are done poaching, carefully remove them from the water using a slotted spoon and drain any excess water.
Place one poached egg on top of each slice of avocado toast.
Season the poached eggs with a sprinkle of salt and pepper, and add any optional toppings you like, such as red pepper flakes, sliced tomatoes, crumbled feta cheese, or chopped fresh herbs.
Serve the avocado toast with poached egg immediately, while the eggs are still warm.
Enjoy your delicious and satisfying breakfast or brunch!

This avocado toast with poached egg is not only tasty but also packed with healthy fats, protein, and fiber, making it a nutritious way to start your day. Feel free to customize the recipe with your favorite toppings or seasonings to suit your taste preferences.

Protein waffles with Greek yogurt topping

Ingredients:

For the waffles:

- 1 cup all-purpose flour or whole wheat flour
- 1 scoop (about 1/4 cup) protein powder (vanilla or unflavored works well)
- 1 tablespoon baking powder
- 1/4 teaspoon salt
- 2 large eggs
- 1 cup milk (dairy or plant-based)
- 2 tablespoons melted butter or oil
- 1 teaspoon vanilla extract (optional)

For the Greek yogurt topping:

- 1 cup Greek yogurt
- 1-2 tablespoons honey or maple syrup (adjust to taste)
- 1 teaspoon vanilla extract (optional)
- Fresh berries or sliced fruit for topping

Instructions:

For the waffles:

Preheat your waffle iron according to the manufacturer's instructions.
In a large mixing bowl, whisk together the flour, protein powder, baking powder, and salt until well combined.
In another bowl, beat the eggs, then stir in the milk, melted butter or oil, and vanilla extract (if using).
Pour the wet ingredients into the dry ingredients and mix until just combined. Be careful not to overmix; a few lumps are okay.
Lightly grease the waffle iron with cooking spray or brush with melted butter or oil.
Pour enough batter onto the center of the preheated waffle iron to cover about 2/3 to 3/4 of the surface area (amount may vary depending on the size of your waffle iron). Close the lid and cook according to the manufacturer's instructions until the waffles are golden brown and crispy.

Remove the waffles from the iron and place them on a wire rack to cool slightly. Repeat with the remaining batter.

For the Greek yogurt topping:

In a small bowl, mix together the Greek yogurt, honey or maple syrup, and vanilla extract (if using) until smooth and well combined.
Taste the mixture and adjust the sweetness if needed by adding more honey or maple syrup.
Spread the Greek yogurt topping over the warm waffles.
Top the waffles with fresh berries or sliced fruit of your choice.

Serve immediately and enjoy your protein-packed waffles with creamy Greek yogurt topping! These waffles are not only delicious but also provide a good balance of protein, carbohydrates, and healthy fats to keep you satisfied and energized throughout the morning.

Turkey sausage and vegetable frittata

Ingredients:

- 6 large eggs
- 1/2 cup milk
- 1 tablespoon olive oil
- 1 small onion, diced
- 1 bell pepper, diced
- 1 cup diced mushrooms
- 2-3 turkey sausages, casings removed and sliced
- Salt and pepper to taste
- 1/2 cup shredded cheese (such as cheddar, mozzarella, or your choice)
- Fresh herbs for garnish (such as parsley or chives)

Instructions:

Preheat your oven to 350°F (175°C).
In a large mixing bowl, whisk together the eggs and milk until well combined.
Season with salt and pepper to taste.
Heat the olive oil in an oven-safe skillet over medium heat.
Add the diced onion and bell pepper to the skillet and sauté until softened, about 3-4 minutes.
Add the diced mushrooms and sliced turkey sausages to the skillet and cook until the mushrooms are tender and the sausage is cooked through, about 4-5 minutes.
Spread the cooked vegetables and sausage evenly across the skillet.
Pour the egg mixture over the vegetables and sausage in the skillet, making sure everything is evenly distributed.
Cook the frittata on the stovetop for 2-3 minutes, or until the edges start to set.
Sprinkle the shredded cheese evenly over the top of the frittata.
Transfer the skillet to the preheated oven and bake for 12-15 minutes, or until the eggs are set and the cheese is melted and bubbly.
Remove the skillet from the oven and let the frittata cool for a few minutes.
Garnish the frittata with fresh herbs, if desired.
Slice the frittata into wedges and serve hot.

Enjoy your delicious turkey sausage and vegetable frittata as a hearty breakfast, brunch, or even a light dinner! It's packed with protein and loaded with flavorful veggies, making it a satisfying and nutritious meal option.

Cottage cheese pancakes with berries

Ingredients:

- 1 cup cottage cheese
- 4 large eggs
- 1/2 cup all-purpose flour
- 1 tablespoon sugar (optional, adjust to taste)
- 1 teaspoon vanilla extract
- 1/2 teaspoon baking powder
- 1/4 teaspoon salt
- Butter or oil for cooking
- Fresh berries (such as strawberries, blueberries, raspberries) for topping
- Maple syrup or honey for drizzling (optional)

Instructions:

In a blender or food processor, combine the cottage cheese, eggs, flour, sugar (if using), vanilla extract, baking powder, and salt. Blend until smooth and well combined.
Heat a non-stick skillet or griddle over medium heat and lightly grease it with butter or oil.
Pour about 1/4 cup of the pancake batter onto the skillet for each pancake. You can adjust the size depending on your preference.
Cook the pancakes for 2-3 minutes, or until bubbles start to form on the surface and the edges look set.
Carefully flip the pancakes with a spatula and cook for an additional 1-2 minutes, or until golden brown and cooked through.
Remove the pancakes from the skillet and repeat with the remaining batter, greasing the skillet as needed.
Serve the cottage cheese pancakes warm, topped with fresh berries.
Drizzle with maple syrup or honey, if desired.
Enjoy your delicious cottage cheese pancakes with berries as a wholesome breakfast or brunch option!

These pancakes are fluffy, protein-packed, and bursting with fruity flavor from the fresh berries. They're a delightful twist on traditional pancakes and make for a satisfying and nutritious meal to start your day. Feel free to customize the recipe with your favorite berries and toppings.

Breakfast quinoa with nuts and honey

Ingredients:

- 1 cup quinoa, rinsed
- 2 cups water or milk (dairy or plant-based)
- Pinch of salt
- 1/4 cup mixed nuts (such as almonds, walnuts, pecans), chopped
- 2 tablespoons honey (or more to taste)
- Optional toppings: sliced fresh fruit (such as bananas, berries, or apples), dried fruit (such as raisins or cranberries), shredded coconut, cinnamon

Instructions:

Rinse the quinoa under cold water using a fine-mesh sieve to remove any bitterness.
In a medium saucepan, combine the rinsed quinoa, water or milk, and a pinch of salt. Bring to a boil over medium heat.
Once boiling, reduce the heat to low, cover, and simmer for about 15-20 minutes, or until the quinoa is cooked and the liquid is absorbed. The quinoa should be tender but still slightly chewy.
Remove the saucepan from the heat and fluff the quinoa with a fork.
Divide the cooked quinoa into serving bowls.
Sprinkle the chopped mixed nuts over the quinoa.
Drizzle honey over the quinoa and nuts.
If desired, add any optional toppings such as sliced fresh fruit, dried fruit, shredded coconut, or a sprinkle of cinnamon.
Stir everything together gently to combine.
Serve the breakfast quinoa warm and enjoy!

This breakfast quinoa with nuts and honey is a delicious and nutritious way to start your day. It's packed with protein, fiber, and healthy fats, providing long-lasting energy to keep you satisfied until your next meal. Feel free to customize the recipe with your favorite nuts, fruits, and toppings to suit your taste preferences.

Egg and vegetable stir-fry

Ingredients:

- 4 large eggs
- 2 cups mixed vegetables (such as bell peppers, broccoli, carrots, snap peas, mushrooms, onions, etc.), sliced or chopped
- 2 cloves garlic, minced
- 1 tablespoon vegetable oil or sesame oil
- 2 tablespoons soy sauce
- 1 tablespoon oyster sauce (optional)
- Salt and pepper to taste
- Cooked rice or noodles for serving (optional)
- Optional garnishes: sliced green onions, sesame seeds, chopped cilantro

Instructions:

In a small bowl, beat the eggs and season with a pinch of salt and pepper.
Heat the vegetable oil or sesame oil in a large skillet or wok over medium-high heat.
Add the minced garlic to the hot oil and stir-fry for about 30 seconds until fragrant.
Add the mixed vegetables to the skillet and stir-fry for 3-5 minutes, or until they are slightly tender but still crisp.
Push the vegetables to one side of the skillet and pour the beaten eggs into the empty space.
Allow the eggs to cook undisturbed for a minute or so until the edges start to set. Then gently scramble the eggs with a spatula until they are cooked through.
Once the eggs are cooked, mix them together with the vegetables in the skillet.
Add soy sauce and oyster sauce (if using) to the skillet and toss everything together until well combined.
Taste and adjust the seasoning with salt and pepper if needed.
Remove the skillet from heat and serve the egg and vegetable stir-fry hot, either on its own or over cooked rice or noodles.
Garnish with sliced green onions, sesame seeds, or chopped cilantro if desired.
Enjoy your delicious egg and vegetable stir-fry!

This dish is quick, easy, and versatile, making it perfect for a healthy weeknight dinner. Feel free to customize the recipe by adding your favorite vegetables or adjusting the seasonings to suit your taste preferences.

Greek yogurt with protein granola and sliced banana

Ingredients:

- 1 cup Greek yogurt (plain or flavored, your choice)
- 1/4 cup protein granola (store-bought or homemade)
- 1 ripe banana, sliced

Instructions:

Spoon the Greek yogurt into a serving bowl.
Sprinkle the protein granola over the Greek yogurt.
Arrange the sliced banana on top of the granola.
Serve immediately and enjoy your delicious and nutritious Greek yogurt with protein granola and sliced banana!

This breakfast or snack option is packed with protein, fiber, and vitamins, making it a satisfying and energizing choice to start your day or refuel after a workout. Feel free to customize the recipe by adding other toppings such as berries, nuts, seeds, or a drizzle of honey or maple syrup for extra sweetness.

Spinach and cheese frittata

Ingredients:

- 6 large eggs
- 1/4 cup milk
- Salt and pepper, to taste
- 1 tablespoon olive oil
- 2 cups fresh spinach leaves, washed and roughly chopped
- 1/2 cup shredded cheese (such as cheddar, mozzarella, or your favorite)
- Optional: additional toppings like diced tomatoes, chopped bell peppers, sliced mushrooms, or cooked bacon or ham

Instructions:

Preheat your oven to 350°F (175°C).
In a mixing bowl, whisk together the eggs, milk, salt, and pepper until well combined.
Heat the olive oil in an oven-safe skillet over medium heat.
Add the chopped spinach to the skillet and cook until wilted, about 2-3 minutes.
Pour the whisked egg mixture into the skillet, making sure the spinach is evenly distributed.
Sprinkle the shredded cheese over the top of the egg mixture.
If desired, add any additional toppings evenly over the cheese.
Let the frittata cook on the stovetop for 3-4 minutes, until the edges start to set.
Transfer the skillet to the preheated oven and bake for 12-15 minutes, or until the frittata is set in the center and the top is golden brown.
Remove the skillet from the oven and let the frittata cool for a few minutes before slicing.
Slice the frittata into wedges and serve warm.

Enjoy your delicious spinach and cheese frittata as a hearty breakfast, brunch, or even a light dinner! It's packed with protein, vitamins, and minerals from the eggs and spinach, and the cheese adds a creamy and flavorful touch. Feel free to customize the recipe with your favorite toppings or seasonings.

Breakfast sandwich with egg, cheese, and turkey bacon

Ingredients:

- 6 large eggs
- 1/4 cup milk or cream
- Salt and pepper, to taste
- 1 tablespoon olive oil
- 2 cups fresh spinach, chopped
- 1/2 cup shredded cheese (cheddar, mozzarella, or your choice)

Instructions:

Preheat your oven to 350°F (175°C).
In a mixing bowl, whisk together the eggs, milk or cream, salt, and pepper until well combined.
Heat olive oil in an oven-safe skillet over medium heat.
Add the chopped spinach to the skillet and sauté until wilted.
Pour the egg mixture into the skillet and sprinkle the shredded cheese evenly over the top.
Cook for 3-4 minutes, until the edges start to set.
Transfer the skillet to the preheated oven and bake for 10-12 minutes, or until the frittata is set in the center and the cheese is melted and bubbly.
Remove from the oven and let it cool for a few minutes before slicing.
Slice the frittata into wedges and serve hot.

Breakfast Sandwich with Egg, Cheese, and Turkey Bacon

Ingredients:

- 2 English muffins, split and toasted
- 2 large eggs
- 2 slices of cheese (cheddar, Swiss, or your choice)
- 4 slices of turkey bacon
- Salt and pepper, to taste
- Butter or oil for cooking

Instructions:

Heat a skillet over medium heat and cook the turkey bacon until crisp. Remove from the skillet and set aside.
In the same skillet, melt a little butter or heat some oil. Crack the eggs into the skillet and cook until the whites are set but the yolks are still runny, or to your desired doneness. Season with salt and pepper.
While the eggs are cooking, place a slice of cheese on each English muffin half.
Once the eggs are cooked, place one egg on each English muffin half.
Top each egg with two slices of turkey bacon.
Close the sandwiches with the remaining English muffin halves.
Serve hot and enjoy your delicious breakfast sandwiches!

These recipes are both versatile and easy to customize according to your taste preferences. They make for hearty and satisfying breakfast options that are perfect for starting your day right!

Almond butter and banana smoothie

Ingredients:

- 1 ripe banana, peeled and sliced
- 2 tablespoons almond butter
- 1 cup almond milk (or any milk of your choice)
- 1 tablespoon honey or maple syrup (optional, for sweetness)
- 1/2 teaspoon vanilla extract (optional, for flavor)
- Handful of ice cubes (optional, for a colder smoothie)
- Optional add-ins: 1 tablespoon chia seeds, 1 tablespoon flaxseed meal, 1 scoop protein powder

Instructions:

Place the sliced banana, almond butter, almond milk, honey or maple syrup (if using), vanilla extract (if using), and any optional add-ins into a blender.
If desired, add a handful of ice cubes to the blender to make the smoothie colder and thicker.
Blend all the ingredients together until smooth and creamy. If the smoothie is too thick, you can add more almond milk to reach your desired consistency.
Taste the smoothie and adjust the sweetness or flavorings if needed.
Once the smoothie is blended to your liking, pour it into glasses and serve immediately.

This almond butter and banana smoothie is creamy, delicious, and packed with nutrients from the banana and almond butter. It's a great way to start your day or refuel after a workout. Feel free to customize the recipe by adding your favorite ingredients or adjusting the quantities to suit your taste preferences. Enjoy!

Quinoa breakfast muffins with ham and cheese

Ingredients:

- 1 cup cooked quinoa
- 1 cup diced cooked ham
- 1 cup shredded cheese (cheddar, mozzarella, or your choice)
- 1/4 cup chopped green onions (optional)
- 4 large eggs
- 1/4 cup milk
- Salt and pepper to taste
- Cooking spray or muffin liners

Instructions:

Preheat your oven to 375°F (190°C). Grease a muffin tin with cooking spray or line with muffin liners.
In a large mixing bowl, combine the cooked quinoa, diced ham, shredded cheese, and chopped green onions (if using). Stir to combine.
In a separate bowl, whisk together the eggs and milk. Season with salt and pepper to taste.
Pour the egg mixture over the quinoa mixture in the bowl. Stir until everything is well combined and evenly coated.
Spoon the mixture evenly into the prepared muffin tin, filling each muffin cup about 3/4 full.
Bake in the preheated oven for 20-25 minutes, or until the muffins are set and golden brown on top.
Remove the muffin tin from the oven and let the muffins cool for a few minutes before removing them from the tin.
Serve the quinoa breakfast muffins warm or at room temperature. Enjoy!

These quinoa breakfast muffins are loaded with protein and make for a filling and satisfying meal. They can be stored in an airtight container in the refrigerator for a few days and reheated in the microwave for a quick and easy breakfast option throughout the week. Feel free to customize the recipe by adding other ingredients such as diced vegetables, herbs, or spices to suit your taste preferences.

Protein oats with almond milk and sliced almonds

Ingredients:

- 1/2 cup rolled oats (old-fashioned oats)
- 1 cup almond milk (or any milk of your choice)
- 1 scoop protein powder (vanilla or unflavored)
- 1 tablespoon sliced almonds
- Optional toppings: fresh fruit (such as berries, banana slices), nut butter (such as almond butter), honey or maple syrup for sweetness, cinnamon, chia seeds

Instructions:

In a small saucepan, combine the rolled oats and almond milk.
Bring the mixture to a gentle simmer over medium heat, stirring occasionally.
Once the oats start to absorb the liquid and soften, reduce the heat to low.
Stir in the protein powder until well combined. Continue to cook for another 2-3 minutes, or until the oats reach your desired consistency.
Remove the saucepan from the heat and transfer the protein oats to a serving bowl.
Sprinkle the sliced almonds over the top of the oats.
If desired, add any optional toppings such as fresh fruit, nut butter, honey or maple syrup, cinnamon, or chia seeds.
Stir everything together gently to combine.
Serve the protein oats warm and enjoy!

This protein oats recipe is highly customizable, so feel free to adjust the ingredients and toppings to suit your taste preferences. It's a great way to start your day with a nutritious and energizing breakfast that will keep you feeling satisfied and full of energy until your next meal.

Egg white breakfast burrito with salsa and avocado

Ingredients:

- 2 large egg whites
- 1 large whole wheat or flour tortilla
- 1/4 cup shredded cheese (cheddar, Monterey Jack, or your choice)
- 2 tablespoons salsa
- 1/4 avocado, sliced
- Salt and pepper to taste
- Optional toppings: chopped fresh cilantro, diced tomatoes, sliced jalapeños, sour cream

Instructions:

In a small bowl, whisk the egg whites until frothy. Season with salt and pepper to taste.
Heat a non-stick skillet over medium heat. Pour the whisked egg whites into the skillet and cook, stirring occasionally, until they are fully cooked and scrambled.
Warm the tortilla in the skillet or in the microwave for a few seconds until it is pliable.
Place the cooked egg whites in the center of the tortilla, leaving some space around the edges.
Sprinkle the shredded cheese over the egg whites.
Spoon the salsa over the cheese.
Arrange the sliced avocado on top of the salsa.
If desired, add any optional toppings such as chopped fresh cilantro, diced tomatoes, or sliced jalapeños.
Fold the sides of the tortilla over the filling, then roll it up tightly to form a burrito.
Serve the egg white breakfast burrito immediately and enjoy!

This egg white breakfast burrito is packed with protein, fiber, and healthy fats from the egg whites, avocado, and cheese. It's a delicious and satisfying meal that's perfect for breakfast or brunch. Feel free to customize the recipe by adding other ingredients such as cooked vegetables, beans, or grilled chicken to suit your taste preferences.

Cottage cheese and spinach omelette

Ingredients:

- 2 large eggs
- 1/4 cup cottage cheese
- 1/2 cup fresh spinach leaves, chopped
- 1 tablespoon olive oil or butter
- Salt and pepper to taste
- Optional fillings: diced tomatoes, sliced mushrooms, chopped bell peppers, shredded cheese

Instructions:

In a mixing bowl, beat the eggs until well combined. Season with salt and pepper to taste.
Stir in the cottage cheese and chopped spinach leaves until evenly distributed.
Heat the olive oil or butter in a non-stick skillet over medium heat.
Pour the egg mixture into the skillet, spreading it out evenly.
Cook the omelette for 2-3 minutes, or until the edges start to set and the bottom is lightly golden.
If using any optional fillings, sprinkle them evenly over one half of the omelette.
Carefully fold the other half of the omelette over the filling to form a half-moon shape.
Cook for another 1-2 minutes, or until the omelette is cooked through and the filling is heated.
Slide the omelette onto a plate and serve hot.

This cottage cheese and spinach omelette is a nutritious and satisfying breakfast or brunch option. It's packed with protein from the eggs and cottage cheese, as well as vitamins and minerals from the spinach. Feel free to customize the recipe by adding your favorite fillings or toppings, such as diced tomatoes, sliced mushrooms, chopped bell peppers, or shredded cheese. Enjoy!

Greek yogurt pancakes with blueberries

Ingredients:

- 1 cup all-purpose flour
- 1 teaspoon baking powder
- 1/2 teaspoon baking soda
- 1/4 teaspoon salt
- 1 cup Greek yogurt (plain or vanilla)
- 1/4 cup milk (dairy or plant-based)
- 1 large egg
- 2 tablespoons honey or maple syrup
- 1 teaspoon vanilla extract
- 1 cup fresh blueberries (or frozen, thawed)

Instructions:

In a large mixing bowl, whisk together the flour, baking powder, baking soda, and salt.
In another bowl, mix together the Greek yogurt, milk, egg, honey or maple syrup, and vanilla extract until well combined.
Pour the wet ingredients into the dry ingredients and stir until just combined. Be careful not to overmix; a few lumps are okay.
Gently fold in the blueberries.
Heat a non-stick skillet or griddle over medium heat and lightly grease with butter or cooking spray.
Pour about 1/4 cup of batter onto the skillet for each pancake, spreading it out slightly with the back of a spoon if needed.
Cook the pancakes for 2-3 minutes, or until bubbles start to form on the surface and the edges look set.
Flip the pancakes and cook for another 1-2 minutes, or until golden brown and cooked through.
Repeat with the remaining batter, greasing the skillet as needed.
Serve the Greek yogurt pancakes warm with additional blueberries and a drizzle of honey or maple syrup if desired.

These Greek yogurt pancakes are fluffy, moist, and bursting with juicy blueberries. They're a nutritious and delicious breakfast option that's sure to please everyone at the table. Feel free to customize the recipe by adding other fruits, nuts, or spices to suit your taste preferences. Enjoy!

Breakfast salad with hard-boiled eggs and bacon

Ingredients:

For the salad:

- Mixed greens (such as spinach, arugula, or kale)
- 2 hard-boiled eggs, sliced
- 4 slices of bacon, cooked and crumbled
- Cherry tomatoes, halved
- Cucumber, sliced
- Red onion, thinly sliced
- Avocado, sliced (optional)
- Croutons (optional)

For the dressing:

- 2 tablespoons olive oil
- 1 tablespoon balsamic vinegar
- 1 teaspoon Dijon mustard
- Salt and pepper to taste

Instructions:

In a large bowl, combine the mixed greens, sliced hard-boiled eggs, crumbled bacon, cherry tomatoes, cucumber, red onion, and avocado (if using).
In a small bowl, whisk together the olive oil, balsamic vinegar, Dijon mustard, salt, and pepper to make the dressing.
Drizzle the dressing over the salad and toss gently to coat everything evenly.
Serve the breakfast salad immediately, topped with croutons if desired.

This breakfast salad is packed with protein from the eggs and bacon, along with plenty of vitamins and minerals from the vegetables. It's a delicious and nutritious way to start your day on a fresh and healthy note. Feel free to customize the salad with your favorite ingredients or add-ins to suit your taste preferences. Enjoy!

Protein-packed French toast with strawberries

Ingredients:

For the French toast:

- 4 slices whole grain bread
- 4 large eggs
- 1/2 cup milk (dairy or plant-based)
- 1 scoop protein powder (vanilla or unflavored)
- 1 teaspoon vanilla extract
- 1/2 teaspoon ground cinnamon
- Butter or oil for cooking

For serving:

- Fresh strawberries, sliced
- Maple syrup or honey
- Greek yogurt or whipped cream (optional)

Instructions:

In a shallow dish or bowl, whisk together the eggs, milk, protein powder, vanilla extract, and ground cinnamon until well combined.
Heat a non-stick skillet or griddle over medium heat and lightly grease with butter or oil.
Dip each slice of bread into the egg mixture, allowing it to soak for about 20-30 seconds on each side.
Place the soaked bread slices onto the preheated skillet or griddle. Cook for 2-3 minutes on each side, or until golden brown and cooked through.
Once cooked, transfer the French toast slices to serving plates.
Top the French toast with sliced strawberries.
Drizzle maple syrup or honey over the French toast and strawberries.
Optionally, serve with a dollop of Greek yogurt or whipped cream on top.
Serve immediately and enjoy your protein-packed French toast with strawberries!

This recipe provides a protein boost to the classic French toast while incorporating the fresh sweetness of strawberries. It's a delicious and satisfying breakfast option that's perfect for starting your day on a nutritious note. Feel free to customize the recipe with your favorite toppings or additional add-ins such as nuts or shredded coconut.

Veggie and tofu scramble wrap

Ingredients:

For the tofu scramble:

- 1 block of firm tofu, drained and pressed
- 1 tablespoon olive oil
- 1/2 onion, diced
- 1 bell pepper, diced
- 1 cup sliced mushrooms
- 2 cloves garlic, minced
- 1 teaspoon ground turmeric
- 1/2 teaspoon ground cumin
- Salt and pepper to taste

For assembling the wrap:

- Large whole grain tortillas or wraps
- Fresh spinach leaves
- Sliced avocado
- Salsa or hot sauce (optional)

Instructions:

Heat the olive oil in a large skillet over medium heat. Add the diced onion and bell pepper and sauté for 3-4 minutes, or until softened.

Add the sliced mushrooms and minced garlic to the skillet. Cook for an additional 2-3 minutes, or until the mushrooms are tender.

Crumble the tofu into the skillet using your hands or a fork. Stir to combine with the vegetables.

Sprinkle the ground turmeric and ground cumin over the tofu mixture. Stir well to evenly distribute the spices.

Cook the tofu scramble for 5-7 minutes, stirring occasionally, until heated through and any excess moisture from the tofu has evaporated.

Season the tofu scramble with salt and pepper to taste. Adjust the seasoning as needed.

Warm the tortillas or wraps in a dry skillet or microwave for a few seconds to make them more pliable.

To assemble each wrap, place a handful of fresh spinach leaves in the center of a tortilla or wrap.
Spoon a generous portion of the tofu scramble over the spinach leaves.
Top the tofu scramble with sliced avocado.
If desired, add a spoonful of salsa or hot sauce for extra flavor.
Roll up the tortilla or wrap, folding in the sides as you go, to form a tight wrap.
Repeat with the remaining ingredients to make additional wraps.
Slice the wraps in half diagonally, if desired, and serve immediately.

These veggie and tofu scramble wraps are flavorful, nutritious, and satisfying, making them a perfect option for a quick and healthy breakfast, lunch, or dinner. Feel free to customize the fillings with your favorite vegetables or add-ins such as black beans, shredded cheese, or fresh herbs. Enjoy!

Protein-packed overnight oats with chia seeds and nuts

Ingredients:

- 1/2 cup rolled oats
- 1 tablespoon chia seeds
- 1/2 cup Greek yogurt (plain or flavored, depending on preference)
- 1/2 cup milk (dairy or plant-based)
- 1 tablespoon honey or maple syrup (optional, for sweetness)
- 1/4 teaspoon vanilla extract
- 2 tablespoons chopped nuts (such as almonds, walnuts, or pecans)
- Fresh fruits for topping (optional)

Instructions:

In a mason jar or any container with a lid, combine rolled oats, chia seeds, Greek yogurt, milk, honey or maple syrup (if using), and vanilla extract. Stir well to combine all ingredients evenly.

Once the ingredients are mixed, add chopped nuts to the mixture. You can also reserve some nuts for topping later.

Seal the jar tightly with a lid and refrigerate overnight, or for at least 4 hours, to allow the oats and chia seeds to soak and soften.

In the morning, give the oats a good stir. If the mixture is too thick, you can add a splash of milk to reach your desired consistency.

Serve the overnight oats cold, topped with fresh fruits and any additional nuts if desired.

Enjoy your protein-packed breakfast!

Feel free to adjust the sweetness, milk quantity, or any other ingredient according to your taste preferences. This recipe provides a nutritious and filling breakfast option that is rich in protein, fiber, and healthy fats from the nuts and chia seeds.

Turkey and cheese breakfast quesadilla

Ingredients:

- 2 large flour tortillas
- 4 slices of turkey breast
- 1/2 cup shredded cheese (cheddar, Monterey Jack, or any cheese of your choice)
- 2 large eggs
- Salt and pepper to taste
- Optional toppings: salsa, avocado, sour cream, chopped tomatoes, chopped cilantro

Instructions:

Heat a skillet over medium heat. While the skillet is heating up, crack the eggs into a bowl and whisk them together. Season with salt and pepper to taste.
Once the skillet is hot, pour the whisked eggs into the skillet and scramble them until fully cooked. Remove the scrambled eggs from the skillet and set aside.
Place one flour tortilla in the skillet. Layer two slices of turkey breast evenly over one half of the tortilla.
Spread the scrambled eggs over the turkey slices, and then sprinkle the shredded cheese on top.
Fold the tortilla in half over the filling, creating a half-moon shape. Press down gently with a spatula.
Cook the quesadilla for about 2-3 minutes on each side, or until the tortilla is golden brown and the cheese is melted.
Once cooked, remove the quesadilla from the skillet and place it on a cutting board. Let it cool for a minute before slicing it into wedges.
Serve the turkey and cheese breakfast quesadilla hot, with optional toppings such as salsa, avocado, sour cream, chopped tomatoes, or chopped cilantro.

Enjoy your delicious and protein-packed breakfast quesadilla!

Smoked salmon and avocado toast

Ingredients:

- 2 slices of whole grain bread (or bread of your choice)
- 1 ripe avocado
- 100g smoked salmon
- 1 tablespoon lemon juice
- Salt and pepper to taste
- Optional toppings: red onion slices, capers, cherry tomatoes, microgreens, dill

Instructions:

Toast the slices of bread to your desired level of crispiness.
While the bread is toasting, cut the avocado in half, remove the pit, and scoop the flesh into a bowl. Add lemon juice, salt, and pepper to taste. Mash the avocado with a fork until smooth and creamy.
Once the bread is toasted, spread the mashed avocado evenly onto each slice.
Top the avocado toast with smoked salmon slices. You can fold or layer the salmon neatly on top of the avocado.
Garnish the toast with any optional toppings you prefer, such as thinly sliced red onion, capers, halved cherry tomatoes, microgreens, or fresh dill.
Season the toast with an extra sprinkle of salt and pepper if desired.
Serve the smoked salmon and avocado toast immediately, while the bread is still warm.

Enjoy your delicious and satisfying smoked salmon and avocado toast! It's packed with healthy fats, protein, and fiber, making it a perfect choice for a nutritious breakfast or brunch.

Protein-packed banana bread with nuts

Ingredients:

- 2 ripe bananas, mashed
- 2 eggs
- 1/4 cup honey or maple syrup
- 1/4 cup plain Greek yogurt
- 1/4 cup milk (dairy or plant-based)
- 1 teaspoon vanilla extract
- 1 1/2 cups whole wheat flour or almond flour
- 1/4 cup protein powder (vanilla or unflavored)
- 1 teaspoon baking powder
- 1/2 teaspoon baking soda
- 1/2 teaspoon ground cinnamon
- 1/4 teaspoon salt
- 1/2 cup chopped nuts (such as walnuts, almonds, or pecans)

Instructions:

Preheat your oven to 350°F (175°C). Grease a loaf pan or line it with parchment paper.
In a large mixing bowl, combine the mashed bananas, eggs, honey or maple syrup, Greek yogurt, milk, and vanilla extract. Mix until well combined.
In a separate bowl, whisk together the whole wheat flour or almond flour, protein powder, baking powder, baking soda, cinnamon, and salt.
Gradually add the dry ingredients to the wet ingredients, stirring until just combined. Be careful not to overmix.
Gently fold in the chopped nuts until evenly distributed throughout the batter.
Pour the batter into the prepared loaf pan, spreading it out evenly.
Bake in the preheated oven for 50-60 minutes, or until a toothpick inserted into the center comes out clean and the top is golden brown.
Remove the banana bread from the oven and allow it to cool in the pan for 10-15 minutes before transferring it to a wire rack to cool completely.
Once cooled, slice the banana bread and serve. Enjoy it as a tasty and protein-rich snack or breakfast option!

Feel free to customize this recipe by adding other mix-ins such as chocolate chips, dried fruits, or seeds. Store any leftovers in an airtight container at room temperature or in the refrigerator for up to several days.

Egg white and spinach breakfast sandwich

Ingredients:

- 2 whole grain English muffins, sliced and toasted
- 4 large egg whites
- 1 cup fresh spinach leaves
- 1/4 cup shredded cheese (optional)
- Salt and pepper to taste
- Olive oil or cooking spray for greasing the pan

Instructions:

Heat a non-stick skillet over medium heat and lightly grease it with olive oil or cooking spray.

Add the fresh spinach leaves to the skillet and sauté them until wilted, about 1-2 minutes. Remove the spinach from the skillet and set it aside.

In the same skillet, pour in the egg whites. Season with salt and pepper to taste. Allow the egg whites to cook undisturbed for a minute or two, until they begin to set around the edges.

Using a spatula, gently push the edges of the egg whites towards the center of the skillet, allowing the uncooked egg to flow underneath. Continue cooking until the egg whites are fully set and cooked through.

If using shredded cheese, sprinkle it over the cooked egg whites and allow it to melt slightly.

While the egg whites are cooking, toast the whole grain English muffins until golden brown.

To assemble the breakfast sandwiches, place a layer of sautéed spinach on the bottom half of each English muffin.

Carefully slide the cooked egg whites (with or without cheese) on top of the spinach.

Top each sandwich with the other half of the English muffin.

Serve the egg white and spinach breakfast sandwiches immediately, and enjoy!

Feel free to customize your breakfast sandwich by adding other ingredients such as sliced tomatoes, avocado, or cooked turkey bacon for extra flavor and protein.

Breakfast pizza with eggs, spinach, and feta

Ingredients:

- 1 pre-made pizza dough (store-bought or homemade)
- 4 large eggs
- 2 cups fresh spinach leaves
- 1/2 cup crumbled feta cheese
- 1 tablespoon olive oil
- Salt and pepper to taste
- Optional toppings: sliced cherry tomatoes, chopped red onion, cooked bacon or sausage

Instructions:

Preheat your oven to the temperature recommended for your pizza dough (usually around 425°F or 220°C).
Roll out the pizza dough on a lightly floured surface to your desired thickness, then transfer it to a pizza stone or baking sheet lined with parchment paper.
In a skillet, heat the olive oil over medium heat. Add the fresh spinach leaves and sauté until wilted, about 1-2 minutes. Season with salt and pepper to taste.
Spread the wilted spinach evenly over the prepared pizza dough.
Sprinkle the crumbled feta cheese over the spinach layer.
Create four small wells or indentations in the spinach and feta mixture for the eggs.
Carefully crack one egg into each well on the pizza.
Place the pizza in the preheated oven and bake for about 12-15 minutes, or until the crust is golden brown and the egg whites are set.
If desired, add any optional toppings such as sliced cherry tomatoes, chopped red onion, cooked bacon or sausage during the last few minutes of baking.
Once the pizza is cooked to your liking, remove it from the oven and let it cool slightly before slicing.
Serve the breakfast pizza hot, and enjoy!

This breakfast pizza is versatile, so feel free to customize it with your favorite ingredients and seasonings. It's perfect for a weekend brunch or a quick and easy breakfast any day of the week.

Greek yogurt with protein powder and sliced almonds

Ingredients:

- 1 cup Greek yogurt (plain or flavored)
- 1 scoop of your favorite protein powder (vanilla or unflavored)
- 2 tablespoons sliced almonds
- Optional: honey or maple syrup for sweetness, fresh berries for topping

Instructions:

In a bowl, combine the Greek yogurt and protein powder. Stir well until the protein powder is fully incorporated into the yogurt.
Taste the mixture and add sweetener like honey or maple syrup if desired, depending on your preference for sweetness.
Once sweetened (if desired), sprinkle the sliced almonds over the yogurt mixture.
If you prefer, top the yogurt with fresh berries for extra flavor and nutrition.
Enjoy your protein-packed Greek yogurt with protein powder and sliced almonds as a quick and satisfying snack or breakfast option!

This snack is not only delicious but also provides a good balance of protein, healthy fats, and carbohydrates to keep you feeling full and satisfied. Feel free to adjust the ingredients and toppings to suit your taste preferences and dietary needs.

High-protein breakfast cookies with oats and nuts

Ingredients:

- 1 cup rolled oats
- 1/2 cup almond flour or oat flour
- 1/4 cup protein powder (vanilla or unflavored)
- 1/4 cup chopped nuts (such as almonds, walnuts, or pecans)
- 1/4 cup dried fruit (such as raisins, cranberries, or chopped dates)
- 1/4 cup honey or maple syrup
- 1/4 cup nut butter (such as almond butter or peanut butter)
- 1 large egg
- 1 teaspoon vanilla extract
- 1/2 teaspoon cinnamon
- 1/4 teaspoon salt

Instructions:

Preheat your oven to 350°F (175°C). Line a baking sheet with parchment paper or lightly grease it.

In a large mixing bowl, combine the rolled oats, almond flour or oat flour, protein powder, chopped nuts, dried fruit, cinnamon, and salt. Stir to combine.

In a separate microwave-safe bowl, combine the honey or maple syrup and nut butter. Microwave for 20-30 seconds, or until the mixture is melted and smooth.

Add the melted honey or maple syrup mixture, egg, and vanilla extract to the dry ingredients. Stir until all ingredients are well combined and a dough forms. If the dough seems too dry, you can add a splash of milk or water to help bind it together.

Using a cookie scoop or spoon, portion the dough into balls and place them on the prepared baking sheet. Flatten each ball slightly with the palm of your hand to form a cookie shape.

Bake the cookies in the preheated oven for 10-12 minutes, or until the edges are golden brown.

Remove the cookies from the oven and let them cool on the baking sheet for a few minutes before transferring them to a wire rack to cool completely.

Once cooled, store the cookies in an airtight container at room temperature for up to several days, or in the refrigerator for longer freshness.

Enjoy your high-protein breakfast cookies with oats and nuts as a convenient and satisfying morning treat or snack on the go!

Egg muffins with turkey sausage and peppers

Ingredients:

- 6 large eggs
- 1/2 cup diced turkey sausage
- 1/2 cup diced bell peppers (any color)
- 1/4 cup diced onion
- 1/4 cup shredded cheese (cheddar, mozzarella, or your choice)
- Salt and pepper to taste
- Cooking spray or olive oil for greasing the muffin tin

Instructions:

Preheat your oven to 350°F (175°C). Lightly grease a muffin tin with cooking spray or olive oil.

In a skillet over medium heat, cook the diced turkey sausage until browned and cooked through, about 5-7 minutes. Remove from the skillet and set aside.

In the same skillet, add the diced bell peppers and onion. Sauté until the vegetables are softened, about 3-5 minutes. Season with salt and pepper to taste.

In a mixing bowl, whisk together the eggs until well beaten. Season with salt and pepper.

Divide the cooked turkey sausage, sautéed peppers, and onions evenly among the muffin cups in the prepared tin.

Pour the beaten eggs over the turkey sausage and vegetable mixture in each muffin cup, filling them about 3/4 full.

Sprinkle shredded cheese over the top of each egg muffin.

Bake in the preheated oven for 20-25 minutes, or until the egg muffins are set and lightly golden on top.

Remove the muffin tin from the oven and let the egg muffins cool for a few minutes before removing them from the tin.

Serve the egg muffins warm, either immediately or store them in an airtight container in the refrigerator for up to several days. They can be reheated in the microwave for a quick and easy breakfast option.

Enjoy your delicious and protein-packed egg muffins with turkey sausage and peppers!

They're perfect for meal prep and can be customized with your favorite veggies and seasonings.

Cottage cheese and fruit smoothie

Ingredients:

- 1/2 cup cottage cheese (low-fat or regular)
- 1/2 cup frozen mixed berries (such as strawberries, blueberries, and raspberries)
- 1/2 ripe banana
- 1/2 cup milk (dairy or plant-based)
- 1 tablespoon honey or maple syrup (optional, for sweetness)
- 1/2 teaspoon vanilla extract (optional)
- Ice cubes (optional, for a colder smoothie)

Instructions:

Place all the ingredients in a blender.
Blend on high speed until smooth and creamy. If the smoothie is too thick, you can add a little more milk until you reach your desired consistency.
Taste the smoothie and add honey or maple syrup for sweetness, if needed. You can also add vanilla extract for extra flavor, if desired.
If you prefer a colder smoothie, you can add a handful of ice cubes to the blender and blend until smooth.
Once the smoothie reaches your desired consistency and taste, pour it into glasses and serve immediately.
You can garnish the smoothie with additional berries or a slice of banana, if desired.

Enjoy your creamy and nutritious cottage cheese and fruit smoothie! It's packed with protein, vitamins, and antioxidants, making it a great choice for a healthy breakfast or snack.

Spinach and mushroom breakfast burrito

Ingredients:

- 4 large eggs
- 1 cup sliced mushrooms
- 1 cup fresh spinach leaves
- 1/2 cup shredded cheese (cheddar, Monterey Jack, or your choice)
- 4 large flour tortillas
- 2 tablespoons olive oil
- Salt and pepper to taste
- Optional toppings: salsa, avocado slices, sour cream, chopped tomatoes

Instructions:

Heat 1 tablespoon of olive oil in a skillet over medium heat. Add the sliced mushrooms and cook until they release their moisture and become tender, about 5 minutes. Season with salt and pepper to taste. Remove the mushrooms from the skillet and set aside.

In the same skillet, add the remaining tablespoon of olive oil. Add the fresh spinach leaves and sauté until wilted, about 2 minutes. Season with salt and pepper to taste. Remove the spinach from the skillet and set aside.

In a bowl, whisk the eggs together until well beaten. Pour the beaten eggs into the skillet and scramble them over medium heat until cooked through.

Once the eggs are cooked, add the cooked mushrooms and spinach back into the skillet. Stir to combine and heat through.

Warm the flour tortillas in a separate skillet or microwave until soft and pliable.

To assemble the breakfast burritos, divide the egg, mushroom, and spinach mixture evenly among the tortillas. Sprinkle shredded cheese over the top of each filling.

Fold the sides of each tortilla inward, then roll them up tightly to form burritos.

If desired, you can warm the assembled burritos in a skillet over medium heat for a few minutes on each side until the tortillas are lightly toasted and the cheese is melted.

Serve the spinach and mushroom breakfast burritos warm, with optional toppings such as salsa, avocado slices, sour cream, or chopped tomatoes.

Enjoy your delicious and satisfying breakfast burritos filled with spinach and mushrooms! They're packed with flavor and nutrients to fuel your morning.

Protein-packed breakfast quiche with bacon and cheese

Ingredients:

- 1 pie crust (store-bought or homemade)
- 6 large eggs
- 1 cup milk (dairy or plant-based)
- 6 slices bacon, cooked and crumbled
- 1 cup shredded cheese (cheddar, Swiss, or your choice)
- 1/2 cup diced onion
- 1/2 cup diced bell peppers (any color)
- Salt and pepper to taste
- Cooking spray or olive oil for greasing the pie dish

Instructions:

Preheat your oven to 375°F (190°C). Lightly grease a 9-inch pie dish with cooking spray or olive oil.

Roll out the pie crust and press it into the prepared pie dish, trimming any excess crust around the edges.

In a skillet, cook the bacon until crispy. Remove the bacon from the skillet and place it on a paper towel-lined plate to drain excess grease. Once cooled, crumble the bacon into small pieces.

In the same skillet, sauté the diced onion and bell peppers until softened, about 3-5 minutes. Season with salt and pepper to taste.

In a mixing bowl, whisk together the eggs and milk until well combined. Season with salt and pepper to taste.

Spread the cooked onion, bell peppers, and crumbled bacon evenly over the bottom of the pie crust. Sprinkle shredded cheese over the top of the bacon and vegetable mixture.

Carefully pour the egg mixture over the bacon, cheese, and vegetables in the pie crust, ensuring that everything is evenly distributed.

Place the quiche in the preheated oven and bake for 35-40 minutes, or until the center is set and the top is golden brown.

Remove the quiche from the oven and let it cool for a few minutes before slicing and serving.

Serve the protein-packed breakfast quiche warm, and enjoy!

This quiche is a great make-ahead option for breakfast or brunch. You can customize it by adding other ingredients like spinach, mushrooms, or different types of cheese. It's versatile and delicious!

Greek yogurt parfait with granola and berries

Ingredients:

- 1 cup Greek yogurt (plain or flavored)
- 1/2 cup granola (store-bought or homemade)
- 1/2 cup fresh berries (such as strawberries, blueberries, raspberries, or a combination)
- Optional: honey or maple syrup for drizzling, chopped nuts for topping

Instructions:

Start by layering the ingredients in a glass or bowl. Begin with a layer of Greek yogurt at the bottom.
Add a layer of granola on top of the yogurt. You can use your favorite store-bought granola or make your own at home.
Next, add a layer of fresh berries over the granola. You can use a single type of berry or a combination for variety and flavor.
Repeat the layers until you reach the top of the glass or bowl, finishing with a final layer of Greek yogurt.
If desired, drizzle honey or maple syrup over the top for added sweetness.
Garnish the parfait with additional berries and chopped nuts for extra flavor and texture.
Serve the Greek yogurt parfait immediately, and enjoy it as a nutritious and delicious breakfast or snack!

This parfait is highly customizable, so feel free to experiment with different types of yogurt, granola, and fruits based on your preferences. It's a great way to incorporate protein, fiber, and vitamins into your diet while satisfying your sweet tooth.

Breakfast scramble with chicken sausage and vegetables

Ingredients:

- 4 large eggs
- 2 chicken sausages, sliced (you can use pre-cooked chicken sausage)
- 1 bell pepper, diced
- 1 small onion, diced
- 1 cup baby spinach leaves
- 1 tablespoon olive oil
- Salt and pepper to taste
- Optional toppings: shredded cheese, chopped fresh herbs (such as parsley or chives), hot sauce

Instructions:

Heat olive oil in a large skillet over medium heat.
Add diced onion and bell pepper to the skillet. Sauté until softened, about 3-5 minutes.
Add sliced chicken sausage to the skillet and cook until heated through and slightly browned, about 3-4 minutes.
Add baby spinach leaves to the skillet and cook until wilted, about 1-2 minutes.
In a separate bowl, whisk together the eggs until well beaten. Season with salt and pepper to taste.
Push the sausage and vegetable mixture to one side of the skillet and pour the beaten eggs into the empty space.
Allow the eggs to cook undisturbed for a minute or two until the edges start to set. Then, using a spatula, gently scramble the eggs until they are cooked through but still moist.
Once the eggs are cooked, mix them with the sausage and vegetable mixture in the skillet until well combined.
Taste and adjust seasoning if necessary.
Remove the skillet from heat and serve the breakfast scramble hot.
Optionally, top with shredded cheese, chopped fresh herbs, or hot sauce before serving.

Enjoy your delicious breakfast scramble with chicken sausage and vegetables! It's packed with protein and nutrients to keep you energized throughout the morning.

High-protein pumpkin pancakes with Greek yogurt topping

Pumpkin Pancakes:

- 1 cup whole wheat flour or oat flour
- 1/2 cup protein powder (vanilla or unflavored)
- 1 teaspoon baking powder
- 1/2 teaspoon baking soda
- 1 teaspoon ground cinnamon
- 1/2 teaspoon ground ginger
- 1/4 teaspoon ground nutmeg
- 1/4 teaspoon ground cloves
- 1/4 teaspoon salt
- 1 cup pumpkin puree
- 2 large eggs
- 1 cup milk (dairy or plant-based)
- 2 tablespoons maple syrup or honey
- 1 teaspoon vanilla extract
- Cooking spray or butter for greasing the skillet

Greek Yogurt Topping:

- 1 cup Greek yogurt (plain or vanilla)
- 2 tablespoons honey or maple syrup
- 1/2 teaspoon vanilla extract

Instructions:

Pumpkin Pancakes:

In a large mixing bowl, whisk together the whole wheat flour or oat flour, protein powder, baking powder, baking soda, cinnamon, ginger, nutmeg, cloves, and salt.
In another bowl, combine the pumpkin puree, eggs, milk, maple syrup or honey, and vanilla extract. Mix until smooth.
Gradually add the wet ingredients to the dry ingredients, stirring until just combined. Be careful not to overmix; a few lumps are okay.
Heat a skillet or griddle over medium heat and lightly grease with cooking spray or butter.
Pour about 1/4 cup of batter onto the skillet for each pancake. Cook until bubbles form on the surface of the pancake and the edges look set, about 2-3 minutes. Flip and cook for another 1-2 minutes until golden brown and cooked through.
Repeat with the remaining batter, greasing the skillet as needed.

Greek Yogurt Topping:

- In a small bowl, mix together the Greek yogurt, honey or maple syrup, and vanilla extract until well combined.
- Adjust sweetness to taste by adding more honey or maple syrup if desired.

Serving:

- Serve the pumpkin pancakes warm, topped with a dollop of Greek yogurt topping.
- Optionally, you can also drizzle additional honey or maple syrup on top for extra sweetness.
- Enjoy your high-protein pumpkin pancakes with Greek yogurt topping for a delicious and nutritious breakfast!

Feel free to customize these pancakes by adding nuts, seeds, or dried fruits to the batter for extra flavor and texture.

Egg white and vegetable breakfast wrap

Ingredients:

- 2 large whole wheat or spinach tortillas (or any wrap of your choice)
- 4 large egg whites
- 1/4 cup diced bell peppers (any color)
- 1/4 cup diced tomatoes
- 1/4 cup diced onions
- 1/4 cup diced mushrooms
- 1/4 cup baby spinach leaves
- Salt and pepper to taste
- Cooking spray or olive oil for greasing the pan

Optional toppings:

- Salsa
- Avocado slices
- Shredded cheese
- Hot sauce

Instructions:

In a small bowl, whisk the egg whites together until frothy. Season with salt and pepper to taste.
Heat a skillet over medium heat and lightly grease it with cooking spray or olive oil.
Add the diced bell peppers, tomatoes, onions, and mushrooms to the skillet. Sauté until the vegetables are softened, about 3-4 minutes.
Add the baby spinach leaves to the skillet and cook until wilted, about 1-2 minutes.
Push the vegetables to one side of the skillet and pour the whisked egg whites into the empty space.
Allow the egg whites to cook undisturbed for a minute or two until the edges start to set. Then, using a spatula, gently scramble the egg whites until they are cooked through but still moist.
Once the egg whites are cooked, mix them with the sautéed vegetables in the skillet until well combined.
Warm the tortillas in a separate skillet or microwave until soft and pliable.

Divide the egg white and vegetable mixture evenly between the tortillas, placing it in the center of each.
Optionally, add any desired toppings such as salsa, avocado slices, shredded cheese, or hot sauce.
Fold the sides of each tortilla inward, then roll them up tightly to form wraps.
Serve the egg white and vegetable breakfast wraps immediately, and enjoy!

These wraps are highly customizable, so feel free to add any other vegetables or toppings you prefer. They're a great way to start your day with a healthy and delicious breakfast!

Protein-packed banana split with Greek yogurt and nuts

Ingredients:

- 1 ripe banana, split lengthwise
- 1/2 cup Greek yogurt (plain or flavored)
- 2 tablespoons chopped nuts (such as almonds, walnuts, or pecans)
- 2 tablespoons granola
- 2 tablespoons honey or maple syrup (optional, for drizzling)
- Optional toppings: fresh berries, sliced strawberries, shredded coconut, dark chocolate chips

Instructions:

Place the split banana halves in a serving dish or on a plate.
Spoon the Greek yogurt over the banana halves.
Sprinkle chopped nuts and granola over the yogurt.
If desired, drizzle honey or maple syrup over the top for extra sweetness.
Optional: Add any additional toppings such as fresh berries, sliced strawberries, shredded coconut, or dark chocolate chips.
Serve the protein-packed banana split immediately, and enjoy!

This banana split is a delicious and nutritious treat that's perfect for breakfast, snack, or dessert. It's loaded with protein, fiber, and healthy fats from the Greek yogurt and nuts, making it a satisfying and wholesome option to fuel your day. Feel free to customize it with your favorite toppings and enjoy!

www.ingramcontent.com/pod-product-compliance
Lightning Source LLC
LaVergne TN
LVHW081317060526
838201LV00055B/2327